CORNERSTONES OF FREEDOM™

AMERICAN CAPITALISM

BY MICHAEL BURGAN

CHILDREN'S PRESS®
An Imprint of Scholastic Inc.
New York Toronto London Auckland Sydney
Mexico City New Delhi Hong Kong
Danbury, Connecticut

BRINGING HISTORY to LIFE

Content Consultant
James Marten, PhD
Professor and Chair, History Department
Marquette University
Milwaukee, Wisconsin

Library of Congress Cataloging-in-Publication Data

Burgan, Michael.
  American Capitalism/by Michael Burgan.
    p. cm.—(Cornerstones of freedom)
  Includes bibliographical references and index.
  ISBN-13: 978-0-531-23054-1 (lib. bdg.)
  ISBN-13: 978-0-531-28154-3 (pbk.)
  1. Capitalism—United States—History—Juvenile literature. 2. United
States—Commerce—History—Juvenile literature. 3. United
States—Economic conditions—Juvenile literature. I. Title.
  HC103.B7895 2012
  330.12'20973—dc23   2012000484

Photographs © 2013: Alamy Images: 49, 57 bottom (HotNYCNews), cover
(Scott Sinklier/AgStock Images, Inc.); AP Images: 50 (Ben Curtis), 54 (Jason
DeCrow), 28 (North Wind Picture Archives), 51 (Phelan M. Ebenhack);
Corbis Images: 18 (Bettmann), back cover (Bruce Benedict/Transtock), 38
(C.P. Cushing/ClassicStock); Getty Images/Margaret Bourke-White/Time
& Life Pictures: 45; Library of Congress: 33 (D. Bendann/Harper's Weekly),
5 bottom, 32 (Harris & Ewing), 20 (Lewis Wickes Hine), 25 (Marceau), 15
(Thomas Hamilton Crawford/Frost & Reed, Ltd.); National Archives and
Records Administration/Courtesy Ronald Reagan Library/ARC 198512: 46, 57
top; National Geographic Stock/Keystone View Co.: 22; Superstock, Inc.: 55
(Blend Images), 16 (Fotosearch), 8, 17; The Granger Collection: 13 (Robert
Graves), 2, 3, 4 bottom, 5 top, 7, 10, 14, 21, 26, 30, 34, 35, 36, 42, 43; The Image
Works/Underwood Archives: 4 top, 40, 59.

Maps by XNR Productions, Inc.

Did you know that studying history can be fun?

BRING HISTORY TO LIFE by becoming a history investigator. Examine the evidence (primary and secondary source materials); cross-examine the people and witnesses. Take a look at what was happening at the time—but be careful! What happened years ago might suddenly become incredibly interesting and change the way you think!

Contents

4

An Early Capitalist at Work

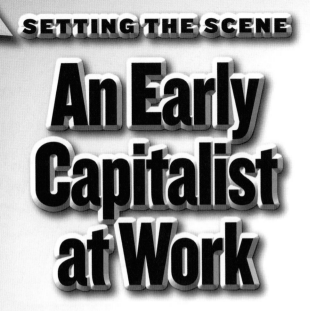

Christopher Leffingwell was a Connecticut merchant who made money by trading goods overseas. He knew a good chance to make money when he saw it. During the 1760s, many American colonists preferred to buy goods made in North America rather than ones **imported** from Great Britain. Leffingwell set up a paper mill and sold his products to Connecticut newspapers.

Leffingwell was a capitalist. Capitalists put their money into businesses in hopes that they will become successful and make more money later on. However, unsuccessful businesses often result in a loss of money. Taking such risks is called investing. Investing is the heart of a capitalist **economy**, such as the one that exists in the United States.

By investing, capitalists help create jobs for workers and produce goods for **consumers** to buy. Workers are

LEFFINGWELL PRODUCED GOODS

consumers, too. They buy goods using the wages they earn from business owners.

The drive for profits sometimes leads people to break the law or act in harmful ways. Capitalists need the freedom to invest in the economy as they choose. Yet the government sometimes limits their actions to protect workers, consumers, or the environment. In many ways, the history of the United States has been about finding a balance between these freedoms and limitations.

Paper mills and other businesses helped drive the colonial economy in the years leading up to the Revolutionary War.

SUCH AS CHOCOLATE AND WOOL CLOTH

CHAPTER 1

BUILDING AMERICAN CAPITALISM

In 1607, in Virginia, colonists founded Jamestown, the first permanent English settlement in North America.

ENGLISH SETTLERS CAME TO
Massachusetts in the 17th century seeking
religious freedom. But most of them, like the early
English settlers in Virginia, also wanted to make
money. The founders of those colonies were part
owners of joint-stock companies. With these
companies, people jointly invested money in the
colonies. They shared any profits that were made
selling the crops and natural resources produced
by the colonies. Some of the investors moved
to North America to start the colonies. Others
remained in England.

Settlers in Virginia grew a new type of tobacco that became extremely popular back in England.

The Mercantile System

In Virginia, tobacco became the main source of profits for colonists and English investors. New England's early economy was based on products such as cod and lumber. Over time, other American colonies developed their own resources to make money for investors.

The colonists were not totally free to pursue their economic interests. Great Britain controlled how goods were bought and sold in its growing colonies. European

rulers believed their governments needed as much gold and silver as possible. They sold as many goods overseas as they could to earn these precious metals. They also imported as few foreign goods as possible, because **domestic** goods were less expensive. Such economic goals were part of the mercantile system.

American colonists played a role in this system but were limited as to how they could expand their own economy. British laws required that certain colonial goods, such as tobacco, could only be shipped to England or its colonies, not to foreign nations. Most of the colonies' imports had to come from England. Imports and **exports** both had to be carried on British ships.

During the early 18th century, the British government added new limits on what the Americans could export. Items such as wool, iron, and hats could be sold only to the British. In 1733, a new law put a type of tax, called a duty, on molasses imported from non-British colonies in the West Indies. This forced colonists to purchase their molasses from British sources. Such trade laws enforced mercantilism by ensuring that profits flowed into Great Britain rather than the colonies.

Growing Tensions

Capitalists follow certain basic rules to make profits. They try to keep their workers' wages low. They also try to reduce the costs of their supplies. Keeping costs low leads to larger profits. Molasses was an important supply for colonial merchants, who turned it into rum. To

avoid paying the duty on this key ingredient, they began smuggling, or illegally importing, it into the colonies. Over the next few decades, smuggling became a major issue between British officials and colonial merchants. The British wanted the colonists to obey the law and pay duties. The colonists believed that they were being treated unfairly, as British merchants didn't always have to pay the same duties. Colonists wanted the freedom to make as much profit as they could.

After 1763, Great Britain began trying harder to stop the smuggling. It also attempted to raise more taxes in the colonies. Both efforts sometimes led to conflict. The Stamp Act of 1765 raised the cost of doing business for many colonists. It placed a tax on almost all papers and documents. Colonists protested the tax so forcefully that it was soon repealed. In the years that followed, more colonists resisted British efforts to raise taxes. Patriots believed that they were being denied their basic freedoms and rights. Many colonists wanted the right to conduct business freely. The conflict with Great Britain soon reached a breaking point.

The Handbook of Early Capitalism

In 1776, the United States officially declared its independence from Great Britain. That same year, a Scottish economist named Adam Smith published *The Wealth of Nations*. This book was a major influence on Americans and others interested in the benefits of capitalism.

Smith studied the market, or the overall exchange of goods and services in an economy. People buy and sell their labor as well as goods. Smith believed that the best market is a free market shaped by the supply of and demand for certain items. If everyone wants cocoa but supply is limited, its price rises. The price falls if demand falls or the supply increases.

The cost of labor also rises and falls depending on supply and demand. If only a few skilled carpenters were in a town, they could earn more money than if many carpenters were competing for the same jobs. Smith saw

Adam Smith's work outlined many of the principles at the heart of the U.S. economy.

YESTERDAY'S HEADLINES

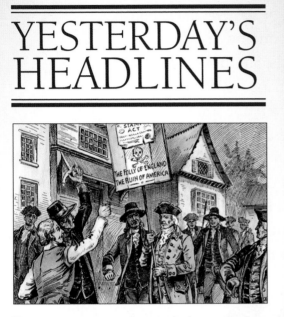

To protest economic restrictions coming from Great Britain, colonial merchants sometimes boycotted, or refused to buy, many British goods. This public statement of 1768 outlines a Boston boycott:

"Having taken into consideration the deplorable situation of the trade ... and the large sums collected by the officers of the customs for duties on goods imported ... and restrictions laid on the trade by several late Acts of Parliament ... we will not send for or import any kinds of goods or merchandise from Great Britain, either on our own account, or on commissions, or any otherwise, from the 1st of January 1769 to the 1st of January 1770."

an "invisible hand" at work in the free market. No one person controlled the cost of goods or labor. Prices changed as conditions in the market changed.

Smith also saw basic human behavior as a key to capitalism. People usually do what best serves their own interests. Making money so they can buy things they like is one part of self-interest. As different people compete to make money, they find better ways of making products or creating new ones. Competition and the invisible hand create changes that help society as a whole. Smith believed that the best way to improve society was to end the mercantile system's limits on trade and manufacturing.

Alexander Hamilton's writings about the U.S. economy helped make him an influential politician.

A Role for Government

Smith did not use the word *capitalism* in his book. That word wasn't used until the 19th century. American merchants and manufacturers were capitalists at heart, though. They welcomed the idea of being free to pursue profits. Still, some early U.S. leaders believed the government should play a role in the economic system.

In the 1780s, Alexander Hamilton wrote about the economic future of the new United States. He agreed with Smith that self-interest in the market was good. He also

The full title of Adam Smith's historic work is *An Inquiry into the Nature and Causes of the Wealth of Nations*. The original two volumes published during Smith's life filled more than 1,000 pages. See page 60 for a link to read the entire work online.

knew that for the country to grow, it needed money from foreign investors. The government could play a role in bringing that money to U.S. businesses. Hamilton became the first secretary of the Department of the Treasury in 1789. He wanted the government to issue bonds. Bonds are certificates sold to investors. The investors eventually

Governments issue bonds in order to borrow money from investors.

receive back the amount they paid, plus a profit called **interest**. In the meantime, the government can use the investors' money. Foreign investors often put the money they earned from bonds into U.S. businesses.

The U.S. economy received more help from the government during the early 1800s. State governments paid for roads and canals, so merchants could easily move their goods across the growing country. The federal government began collecting protective tariffs, which were high taxes on certain imported goods. This caused similar goods made in America to be more affordable. U.S. manufacturers were able to sell more goods, hire more workers, and make profits they could invest in new businesses. The U.S. economy grew even more as capitalism around the world entered a new phase.

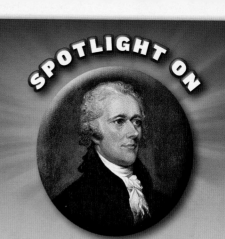

SPOTLIGHT ON

Alexander Hamilton

Alexander Hamilton came to America from the Caribbean island of St. Croix in 1772. He quickly impressed other colonists with his intelligence and his devotion to the Patriot cause. During the revolution, he served as a top aide to General George Washington and fought bravely in several key battles. After the war, Hamilton argued for creating a new central government for the United States. He helped start the first national bank, and he promoted **commercial** development in the new country. In 1804, Hamilton was killed in a duel with Vice President Aaron Burr. Today, Hamilton is remembered as one of the great economic thinkers in early U.S. history.

CHAPTER 2

INDUSTRY ON THE RISE

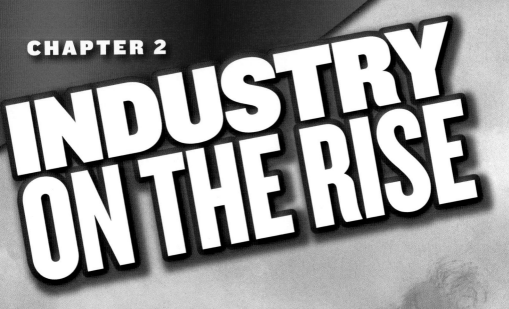

Moses Brown and Samuel Slater helped begin a new era in the U.S. economy with the opening of their cotton mill in Rhode Island.

THE RUSHING WATERS OF THE

Blackstone River turned a giant wooden wheel. The wheel was connected to machinery inside a brick factory. The machinery turned rows of wooden pegs called spindles. On the spindles, cotton was spun into thread.

Rhode Island merchant Moses Brown invested the money to build this cotton mill. It was the first of its kind in the United States. Brown needed the help of a man named Samuel Slater to get the machinery running. Slater had worked in similar mills in Great Britain. The British government had made it illegal to sell the equipment to make **textiles**. It did not want any competition with its own mills. But Slater had memorized how the machines were made. In 1790, he helped Brown open his mill. More textile mills soon sprang up across New England. The first major industry in the United States was born.

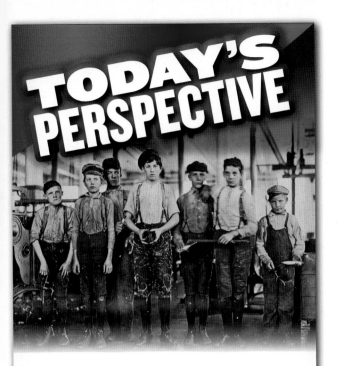

Mills often hired children to run machinery. Some were as young as five years old. For thousands of years, children had worked with their families on farms. Most Americans saw nothing wrong with children working. The children made money their families could use, and many state governments did not require children to attend school. Attitudes toward child labor began to change by the 20th century. States saw the need for children to be educated. Some people saw that children faced harmful working conditions in factories. Today, the U.S. government limits the number of hours that children under 16 years old can work. It also prevents them from working dangerous jobs such as mining or running heavy equipment.

Creating Industrial Capitalism

The first modern capitalists created joint-stock companies to buy and sell goods overseas. The most valuable goods included spices from Asia, furs, and cloth. Many Dutch or English joint-stock companies had **monopolies**. This means just one company controlled all the trade in a region. Such overseas trade has been called merchant capitalism. Its lack of competition made it different from what most people today think of as capitalism. True competition began between businesses backed by private investors as Europe's economy became industrialized.

English textile mills produced the materials used to make clothing and other useful products.

The rise of large industries relying on water or steam power began in England during the late 1700s. The appearance of textile mills marked the start of the Industrial Revolution. Many people began leaving farms to work in factories. Improvements in agricultural technology and methods made this possible. Fewer farmers could produce more crops than they had in previous centuries.

This new economic phase is known as industrial capitalism. It led to great changes in society. Capitalists invested large amounts of money to build mills and other factories. They also made large profits. Bigger and

Factories used specialized machinery to create their products.

better machines helped reduce the cost of making goods. Machines could do more work than people could and didn't need to rest.

Companies also began to specialize in one or two processes. Early mill owners made their own machinery and also sold textiles to stores. As companies grew, they bought machines from other companies that only made heavy equipment. Companies began selling their goods to merchants called wholesalers. Wholesalers then sold the goods to stores at a slightly higher price. Steam-powered ships and trains made it easier for business owners to ship their goods over long distances. This enabled them to sell to a larger group of customers.

For centuries, most people had earned money selling things they made themselves. Now, for the first time,

workers were paid wages for their jobs. In the past, people or families usually completed all the steps to turn raw materials into finished products. Now they often did only one part of the manufacturing process.

Many workers lost the freedom to do as they wished during the workday. Company owners expected them to start working at a particular time and keep working until the end of the day, with limited breaks. Some capitalists built towns for their workers outside the mills. They continued to watch what the workers did even after they left work for the day. The owners did not want employees who drank too much, broke the law, or did anything else that might negatively affect their work.

Early Industry in the United States

The Industrial Revolution arrived slightly later in the United States than it did in Great Britain. Textile manufacturing was the first major industry in the United States. Another early industry was gun manufacturing. Beginning in the 1820s, machines turned out identical parts for the guns faster than workers could by hand. Because they were exactly alike, each gun part could be easily replaced by another if something broke. The use of machine-made, interchangeable parts spread to other U.S. industries. This helped lower manufacturing costs and boost profits at various companies. Lower costs also meant more consumers were able to buy such goods.

The French political scientist Alexis de Tocqueville visited the United States during the 1830s. He offered Europeans this view on U.S. business activity:

"No people in the world have made such rapid progress in trade and manufactures as the Americans.... In the United States, the greatest undertakings and **speculations** are executed without difficulty, because the whole population are engaged in productive industry, and because the poorest as well as the most opulent [richest] members of the commonwealth are ready to combine their efforts for these purposes."

The railroad industry came to the United States in the 1830s. By 1860, the country had about 30,000 miles (48,000 kilometers) of tracks. Trains carried passengers and goods over large areas of the country. New industries arose to support the railroads. Steam engines needed coal. Iron and steel had to be turned into tracks and trains. Capitalists in these industries, such as J. P. Morgan and Andrew Carnegie, became some of the richest people in America.

The Corporation

Building large mills or creating big businesses was not easy for a single investor. Instead, U.S. investors came together to create corporations. In a corporation, a number of investors put up money and receive profits based on their share of the company's worth. If the company loses money, the investors are all responsible for a similar share of its **debt**.

A few corporations formed during colonial times, but they became much more common during the 1800s. Corporations stood separate from their investors. Individual shareholders might die, but the corporation survived. Also, the owners did not have to do the day-to-day business activities. They could hire lawyers and managers to run most affairs. Two corporations could also come together, or merge, to form one large corporation. A merger could give the new, larger company more money to invest and increase its production, leading to lower costs.

Andrew Carnegie made millions of dollars in the steel industry.

Investors gather on the trading floor of the New York Stock Exchange to buy and sell stocks.

Companies of all sizes could sell stocks to new investors in a stock market. Stocks are shares in the ownership of a company. Investors could buy and sell stocks as they chose, hoping to make a profit. Stock markets, or exchanges, first appeared in Europe. America's first stock exchange opened in Philadelphia, Pennsylvania, in 1791. Two years later, New York investors created what later became the New York Stock Exchange. They met on Wall Street in the southern part of Manhattan. Today, "Wall Street" usually refers to major New York banks and financial companies, whether they are actually located on the street or not.

A FIRSTHAND LOOK AT
EDISON'S PATENT APPLICATION

Many capitalists are also inventors. To make sure no one else makes money from their invention, they fill out a legal form called a patent application. In 1880, the great inventor Thomas Edison received a patent for a lightbulb he invented. See page 60 for a link to view his patent application online.

Growing Larger

By the 1840s, Americans had settled along the Pacific coast. These settlements provided new opportunities for capitalists. The discovery of gold in California in 1848 led to a gold rush. Tens of thousands of people flocked to the state from all over the world. In the decades that followed, mining became a big business in many parts of the West. Some capitalists made money mining gold and silver. Others started banks and stores to serve the people who worked in the mines and the new towns that formed around them.

After the Civil War (1861–1865), the country's economy continued to grow. Raising cattle on the grasses of the Great Plains brought wealth to ranchers and meatpacking companies. Railroads brought goods to distant buyers back East.

The great wealth made by some investors during the 1800s did not hide the fact that capitalism can cause problems for some workers and small investors. Soon, more people began to speak out about these issues.

CHAPTER 3

CHALLENGES TO CAPITALISM

The U.S. government aided railroad companies by providing them with land to build tracks across the West.

THE TREMENDOUS SUCCESS of a few capitalists showed that the freedom to invest could make some Americans rich. To keep increasing their wealth, many business owners and investors sought a policy called laissez-faire. *Laissez-faire* is a French term meaning, roughly, "leave it alone." Capitalists wanted the government to keep their taxes low and avoid passing laws that increased their costs.

The Panic of 1837 led to widespread unemployment and other financial difficulties for Americans.

Yet companies welcomed laws that helped them grow. For example, the government gave railroad companies land so they would build railways in the West. The railroad then sold some of the land to settlers. In general, the industrial capitalists wanted policies that would lead to greater profits. They opposed laws that limited their ability to invest or to lower costs. However, many Americans believed laissez-faire was harmful. Industries did not always treat workers and consumers well. During the late 1800s and early 1900s, the call for regulation and workers' rights grew louder.

Recession and Depression

The desire for increased government action sometimes comes during tough times. Capitalism often faces periods of recession. The economy stops growing during a recession. Capitalist companies constantly try to reduce costs. One way to do this is to produce more of a product. As more of a single good is made, production costs fall. Experts call this economies of scale. Once a company has bought its machinery and built a factory, producing larger numbers of an item makes the cost of each item smaller. However, the company has to lower the selling price if supply rises and demand doesn't. Its competitors do the same. Eventually, profits begin to fall.

Owners might begin to reduce wages or lay off workers to try to keep their businesses going. The workers then have less money to spend, so they buy fewer products. More companies face falling sales and profits. The layoffs spread, and the economy enters a recession. An especially bad recession is called a depression.

The United States saw several recessions and depressions during the 1800s. At the time, they were called panics. The Panic of 1837 was partly tied to a banking problem that cut off the flow of money in the economy. British banks stopped investing in U.S. companies because of economic problems at home. U.S. banks then began seeking repayments of loans they had made to Americans. The situation led to a "credit crunch" where people found it hard to borrow money to invest. The president at the time, Martin Van Buren, had a laissez-faire view. He did not take

YESTERDAY'S HEADLINES

In 1894, Jacob Coxey (above) led several hundred protesters in a march from Ohio to Washington, D.C. "Coxey's Army" wanted the government to help people who had lost their jobs. Coxey wrote a speech to give to Congress, but he was arrested for walking on the grass when he arrived at the U.S. Capitol. It would be 50 years before he was finally able to give his speech on the steps of Congress:

"[Congress] should heed the voice of despair and distress that is now coming up from every section of our country ... they should consider the conditions of the starving unemployed of our land, and enact such laws as will give them employment, bring happier conditions to the people, and the smile of contentment to our citizens."

strong steps to end the depression. He said, "The less government interferes with private pursuits, the better for the general prosperity." The economy did not recover fully until 1843.

Another panic hit in 1873. Rail companies had added tens of thousands of miles of tracks and linked the East Coast to the West. But railway investors saw that the country now had more tracks than it needed. Railways laid off workers, sparking a recession.

The roots of the 1893 panic were more complex. Many factors played a part, including falling prices for crops, which hurt farmers, and foreign investors selling their stocks in U.S. companies. People

did not have enough money to buy the goods that companies were making. During the 1890s, more than 10 percent of the U.S. workforce was unemployed for several years in a row.

Workers Respond

During the panics of 1873 and 1893, some workers reacted strongly to the falling wages brought on by worsening economic conditions. They sometimes went on strike, or refused to work unless they received higher pay or better working conditions. These strikes sometimes became violent. An 1877 strike called by

The Great Railroad Strike of 1877 grew violent when U.S. troops confronted the striking workers.

Communism

German philosopher and writer Karl Marx believed the free market did not benefit everyone. The owners of capital always had an advantage over workers, and they grew increasingly rich over time. Meanwhile, workers suffered from the regular recessions and depressions that developed under capitalism. Marx believed that workers had to unite against capitalists to take control of the means of production, such as factories. When capitalism ended, all people in a society would share the sources of production. Marx called this system communism. Communism was never widely popular in the United States. Too many people accepted the rights to own private property and make money through investing.

railroad workers in Baltimore, Maryland, spread to other cities. In 1894, there was a major strike at the Pullman Company, which made railroad cars. President Grover Cleveland sent in U.S. troops to end it.

The strikes were part of a growing demand for workers' rights. Workers and capitalists sometimes disagree on how profits should be shared. Part of the conflict during the 1800s came from new ideas outlined by thinkers such as Karl Marx. The strikes were also the result of unions.

Workers joined unions so they could speak with one voice to their bosses. Unions sought safer working conditions and shorter workdays. Most of all, they sought higher pay for their members.

Strikers sometimes harassed the workers hired to replace them during strikes.

Strikes were the unions' weapon against capitalists who refused their demands. By not working, workers caused companies to lose money. Capitalists often opposed workers' rights to join unions or go on strike.

A FIRSTHAND LOOK AT
"ONLY A WORKINGMAN'S CHILD"

The economic troubles of the 1870s influenced Ned Straight to write songs about workers struggling to survive. His song "Only a Workingman's Child" told about a young girl forced to work to help her family. See page 60 for a link to view the sheet music for the song online.

Growing Too Big

By the end of the 1800s, American capitalism had created some of the largest corporations in the world. In some industries, these companies were formed by mergers. In the oil industry, John D. Rockefeller pushed for what he called consolidation, or bringing all parts of an industry under the control of one company. Rockefeller wanted a monopoly in the oil business. Other capitalists sought monopolies as well.

John D. Rockefeller's Standard Oil Company almost took over the entire U.S. oil industry during the late 1800s and early 1900s.

These huge new companies were sometimes called trusts. Some Americans feared the trusts' power to set prices, rather than letting competition and the invisible hand work as they should. People known as Progressives became active in politics during the late 1800s and early 1900s. Many Progressive causes had originally been taken up by a group known as the Populists. Most Populists were farmers from the Midwest and the South who believed that U.S. laws prevented agriculture from reaching economic equality with industry.

Progressives claimed that men such as Rockefeller and J. P. Morgan stole wealth instead of earning it. One Progressive goal was "trust busting," or breaking up the large corporations that dominated a single industry.

An 1890 law called the Sherman Anti-Trust Act was supposed to end the trusts. The law was not always enforced, and a U.S. Supreme Court decision limited the government's power against the trusts. In 1902, however, President Theodore Roosevelt took one trust to court and won, forcing its breakup. The U.S. government busted more trusts in the next decade, including Rockefeller's Standard Oil trust.

Roosevelt and the Progressives did not oppose the freedom to invest or the freedom of a company to grow large. Roosevelt knew that large companies helped make the United States wealthy. However, critics opposed corporations that tried to limit competition. Even without trusts and monopolies, U.S. corporations would continue to build great wealth for investors.

CHAPTER 4

NEW CHALLENGES

Home appliances such as refrigerators became popular among middle-class Americans during the 1920s.

DURING THE 1920S, THE growing U.S. economy created a new group of consumers known as the middle class. These people earned much less than the rich but much more than the poor. They purchased goods such as radios, cars, and home appliances. These consumers often bought things on credit if they did not have all the money they needed for a product. This means they took out small loans that they paid back over time.

The 1929 stock market crash had a devastating impact on the world economy.

A Boom Turns to Bust

In 1925, President Calvin Coolidge said, "The chief business of the American people is business." Becoming wealthy through capitalism was many Americans' main goal in life. Coolidge also believed that wealth was not the only thing Americans wanted. They also sought peace and to help others live freely. Still, making money was a big part of the 1920s.

World War I (1914–1918) involved several dozen nations. Its high cost hurt the economies of many of those countries. The United States suffered for a time, but its

economy soon began booming again. Still, the roots of capitalism's worst crisis ever were slowly growing.

U.S. farmers increased their production during the war. They continued producing large amounts of crops even after it ended. Prices for the crops fell. Farmers found it hard to pay back loans. Factories started to produce more goods than consumers could buy. Companies began to fire workers, and a recession began.

Hard times hit Wall Street in 1929. Buying stock in U.S. companies was a good investment during the 1920s. The price of most stocks rose, and companies paid **dividends**. Some people borrowed money so they could buy more stocks. They assumed the value of the stocks would keep rising and they would be able to pay off their loans in the future. But stock prices began to fall in October 1929. More investors began to sell, hoping to regain some of what they had paid. The stockbrokers who had loaned money to investors wanted their money repaid. Some investors didn't have the money to pay back the loans. The brokers then couldn't repay money they had borrowed from banks. These events of 1929 are called the stock market crash.

As the economy worsened, people began to rush to banks to withdraw their savings. Some banks didn't have enough money on hand to meet this demand. More than 9,000 banks went out of business between 1930 and 1933. Many people lost all of their savings. World events added to the problem. Many countries, including the United States, set up tariffs that

made it hard for companies to sell goods overseas. Unemployment increased in many nations. The entire world had entered the Great Depression.

Seeking a Solution

Americans elected Franklin Roosevelt president in 1932. Around 25 percent of Americans were out of work when he took office. Roosevelt believed strong government action was the only way to save capitalism in the United States. He encouraged deficit spending, or spending more money than the government took in each year. He wanted to use the money to help the unemployed and create new jobs. In general, people, businesses, and governments try to stay out of debt. Going into debt is the sign of a struggling company. But Roosevelt accepted the ideas of economists

During the Great Depression, lines at unemployment offices often stretched for blocks.

who argued that taking on debt in the short term would boost the U.S. economy.

Roosevelt called his actions the New Deal. The New Deal created Social Security, which gives money to the elderly, the disabled, and some people out of work. Businesses and workers pay a tax to fund this program. The Works Progress Administration put people to work by paying them to do things such as build bridges or create art. Congress passed laws that made it easier for workers to form unions.

The New Deal also placed a large number of new restrictions on businesses and banks. New government organizations were created to oversee the banking industry.

TODAY'S PERSPECTIVE

Today, more people collect Social Security benefits than in the past. People also live longer. As a result, there is less Social Security money to go around. Some people fear the system might break down if the government does not change it. Some politicians have called for getting rid of Social Security. Instead, they suggest that workers take the money they now pay into the system and invest it on their own. Critics argue that wide swings in the stock market mean workers could lose money and not have it when they retire. Keeping Social Security a government program provides a "safety net." However, the government might not always have as much money in the future to pay out as it does now.

Many business leaders opposed these changes, which often included tax increases and a rise in other costs. Some small, middle-class investors were also unhappy with the New Deal. One investor complained about Roosevelt's "merciless attacks" on businesses and said all she wanted was for the president to "balance the budget and reduce taxes." When Roosevelt did try to slow government spending in 1937, the economy fell again.

War and Prosperity

War finally put Americans back to work. In 1939, Germany began World War II (1939-1945) by attacking Poland. The U.S. government began to spend money on manufacturing military equipment. That spending rose even higher when the United States entered the war in 1941. This gave the U.S. economy a huge boost. The regained industrial power of the United States helped to win the war.

Parts of the New Deal remained in place even after the recovery. More Americans accepted the government's role in the economy. Military spending remained high as the country fought wars in Korea and Vietnam. By the 1960s, Americans had built the largest economy in the world. Companies issued more stock and new bonds to attract more investors. They also expanded overseas as more countries built their own healthy middle classes.

A Changing Economy

The new, global economy was good for U.S. companies and capitalists who invested overseas. But the increasing

Under the New Deal, the government created jobs by funding construction projects.

connections to other countries also brought problems. The U.S. economy was powered by oil, which was needed to run vehicles of all kinds, provide heat, and make plastics and other goods. By the early 1970s, the country was relying more and more on foreign oil. Much of it came from the Middle East.

Twice during the decade, some oil-producing countries from that region refused to sell oil to the United States and other nations. The price of gas skyrocketed and added to **inflation**. The high inflation of the late 1970s came during a period when unemployment was also high. Running for president in 1980, Ronald Reagan asked Americans if they

Ronald Reagan believed that the U.S. economy would benefit from a lack of restrictions on businesses and investors.

were better off than they had been four years earlier. Many said no. They chose Reagan to deal with the growing economic problems.

Reagan hoped to return to laissez-faire capitalism. He wanted to reduce taxes and end regulations that raised costs for businesses. Under Reagan, the government tried to lower inflation by raising interest rates. Raising these rates made it more expensive for people to borrow money for large purchases or investments. With less spending, inflation did fall. However, the country also entered another recession.

The economy improved during the mid-1980s, as U.S. investors found new ways to make money. Banks and other financial companies had already begun to play a larger role in U.S. capitalism. They increasingly loaned money to people and businesses seeking to make large investments. At times, financial companies bought and

sold things besides stocks and bonds, such as futures and options. Futures are contracts for selling goods, stocks, or bonds at a certain price at a certain future date. An option is an agreement that gives an investor the right to buy or sell something at a certain price.

Even economists admitted that these financial products were complex. Governments found it hard to watch over how they were used. This era of growing financial capitalism led to great wealth for some investors.

Winners and Losers of the Information Age

The rising importance of computers fueled some of the economy's growth, starting at the end of the 1970s. American capitalism became less focused on making and selling products. Instead, more companies provided services such as banking and selling retail goods. These companies relied on computers to process and store information. The rise of computers led to what is called the information age.

U.S. companies built the technology that made the first computers. These early computers were large enough to fill a room. Starting in the 1970s, several American **entrepreneurs** developed smaller, more powerful computers. The prices for these personal computers fell, and soon millions of people could afford to buy them.

Two of the most important computer entrepreneurs were Steve Jobs and Bill Gates. Jobs helped start Apple Computer, Inc. Apple is famous today for its Macintosh

A FIRSTHAND LOOK AT
STEVE JOBS'S STANFORD SPEECH

Steve Jobs died in 2011 at the age of 56. Several years before his death, he gave a speech to students at Stanford University. That speech reflects some of the ideas that helped him succeed in business. See page 60 for a link to read the speech online.

computers and iPhones. Jobs and his partner, Steve Wozniak, built their first computer in Jobs's garage. Gates wrote computer programs and helped start Microsoft, one of the largest technology companies in the world.

The success of Jobs, Gates, and other young inventors sparked a boom in computers. New technology led to growth in productivity. Raising productivity helps a company lower its costs. It can produce more goods or provide more services using fewer workers.

Even before the personal computer was invented, government scientists and engineers had created the Internet. During the 1990s, the introduction of the World Wide Web made it easy for companies and consumers to connect to the Internet. This widespread use of the Internet led to a new phase of American capitalism based on marketing and selling goods through the Web. Investors rushed to fund new online companies. These "dot-com" companies issued stock and saw their values soar.

As during the 1920s, some investors thought the value would keep rising. However, many of the companies could not make a profit. The rise in their stocks was called a bubble. Like real bubbles, it eventually burst. Stock prices

for many dot-coms fell when the companies could not make money. One example was eToys. In 1999, its shares sold for $84 each. Less than two years later, they were worth only pennies. Some dot-coms, such as eBay and Amazon, survived and are now major companies. Google, which began as a search engine, is now one of the most valuable companies in the world.

New Challenges

The U.S. economy stumbled once again in the early 2000s. The dot-com bubble was partly to blame. So were the terrorist attacks of September 11, 2001. The economy quickly recovered from this recession, but new problems emerged. The country's debt grew as the government cut taxes and increased military spending to fight wars in Iraq and Afghanistan. Then the housing market had its

Bill Gates's contributions to the development of personal computers have made him one of the wealthiest men in the world.

Spotlight On

Outsourcing

U.S. companies have moved many jobs to foreign countries. This process of sending work overseas is called outsourcing. The earliest outsourcing moved factory jobs to foreign countries where labor costs are low. The rise of personal computers has also allowed companies to outsource jobs in computer programming, customer service, and printing. Even law firms and hospitals hire foreign workers. These workers use computers to do research or review documents and images. Outsourcing helps U.S. companies reduce costs, since most foreign workers earn less than Americans doing the same job.

worst crisis since the Great Depression.

The value of homes had soared during the early 2000s. Many buyers thought home prices would keep rising. Some people got **mortgages** for homes that they couldn't afford. But lenders did not care if home buyers couldn't afford to pay back their loans. They were making money on the loans they gave. Some borrowers saw their mortgage rates rise. They couldn't pay the higher rates. The housing bubble burst and caused serious damage to the economy. The United States entered its worst recession since the Great Depression. Other nations felt the effects as well.

Banks began to loan less money. Some businesses found it harder to get money to expand. Unemployment rose, and the number of people who could not afford to

pay the mortgage on their homes also rose. Several financial companies went out of business. Others needed loans from the government to survive. So did two of the nation's three major automakers.

Some Americans complained about using tax dollars to help companies. In capitalism, companies that can't compete go out of business. Better companies make money and survive. Some lawmakers argued that the companies were "too big to fail." Too much money and too many jobs would be lost if they went out of business. The recession ended in 2009, but many Americans could not tell the difference. Housing prices continued to fall, and unemployment remained high. Still, some entrepreneurs used their savings or took out loans to start new businesses. Some companies reported big profits. Despite recessions, people value their freedom to invest as they choose to try to make money.

Many Americans lost their homes during the recession of the late 2000s.

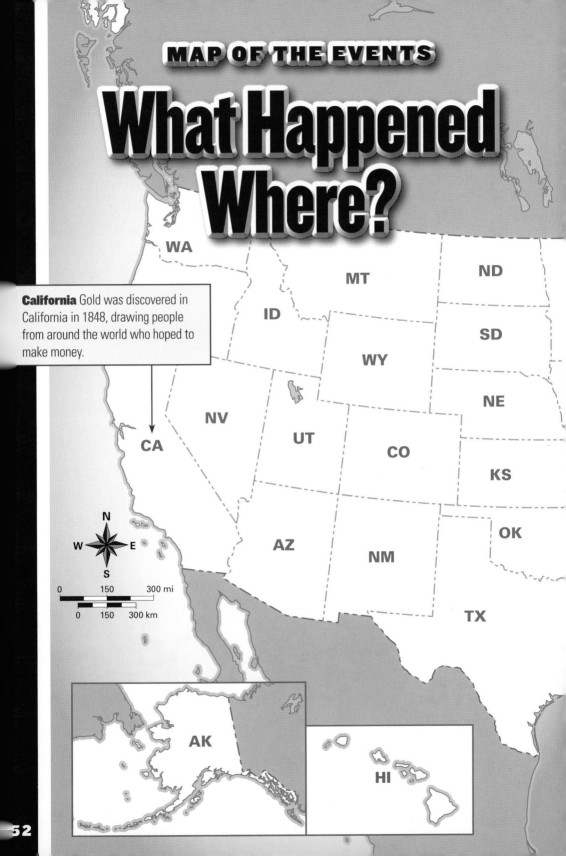

MAP OF THE EVENTS

What Happened Where?

California Gold was discovered in California in 1848, drawing people from around the world who hoped to make money.

WA

MT

ND

ID

SD

WY

NE

NV

UT

CO

KS

CA

N
W E
S

0   150   300 mi

0   150   300 km

AZ

NM

OK

TX

AK

HI

New York City New York City's Wall Street is the heart of the U.S. financial system. In 2011, it was the first site of major protests against the growing income gap between wealthy and average Americans.

Baltimore, Maryland In 1877, Baltimore was the site of a strike by railroad workers protesting a cut in wages. As the strike spread, workers sometimes battled troops and damaged railroad property.

Pawtucket, Rhode Island Samuel Slater and Moses Brown opened the first U.S. textile mill in Pawtucket. Today, visitors can tour a mill that Slater built there in 1790.

MN

WI

MI

NY

VT

NH

MA

Pawtucket

CT

RI

IA

PA

New York City

NJ

OH

Baltimore

Philadelphia

IL

IN

Washington, D.C.

DE

MD

MO

WV

VA

KY

Philadelphia, Pennsylvania Philadelphia served as the nation's capital from 1790 to 1800 and was an early banking center.

NC

TN

SC

AR

AL

GA

MS

Washington, D.C. As the nation's capital, Washington hosts many lobbyists, or people who represent the views of capitalists, workers, and consumers. Lobbyists try to convince politicians to pass laws that protect the interests of their particular group.

LA

FL

What Comes Next?

In 2011, thousands of Americans gathered in New York City to protest the unfair business practices of wealthy capitalists.

The recession of 2007–2009 made people wonder about the future of capitalism in America. Can U.S. companies compete with foreign businesses that have cheaper labor costs? Can there be equality as the middle class becomes poorer and the rich grow richer? Can the needs of all people in society be met when capitalism relies on making profits at any cost?

These questions are often the subject of political debates. The Republican Party generally wants lower taxes and fewer laws that limit business. They oppose increasing government spending to try to create new jobs. Most Democrats realize the country cannot continue to spend more money than it takes in each year. However, they believe the government can play a useful role in the economy.

The role of the government in America's capitalist system will change over time, depending on which party is in control. But several things will remain true. New entrepreneurs will emerge with products or ideas that help others and are profitable, and U.S. companies will continue to be the world leaders in some industries, thanks to the talents of U.S. workers. Whatever its problems, capitalism has given people the freedom to pursue their economic dreams.

In the U.S. economy, people are free to spend their money however they choose.

EVENTUALLY SPREAD TO OVER 100 U.S. CITI

INFLUENTIAL INDIVIDUALS

Adam Smith (1723–1790) was a Scottish thinker who wrote down the basic ideas of capitalism in *The Wealth of Nations*. His ideas formed the basis of much of modern economics.

Alexander Hamilton (1755–1804) argued for a strong national government. He wanted the government to pursue policies that would help investors and businesses.

Samuel Slater (1768–1835) is called the father of the American Industrial Revolution. He helped build the country's first textile mill. He also built a village to house workers at his mill.

Karl Marx (1818–1883) was one of the strongest critics ever of capitalism. He believed workers were treated poorly and needed to take control of the means of production. His ideas were the basis of communism.

Andrew Carnegie (1835–1919) came to the United States as a poor Scottish immigrant. He used his intelligence and drive to create the largest steel company in America and become, for a time, the richest person in the country. He used some of his wealth to open public libraries.

J. P. Morgan (1837–1913) entered banking during the 1860s and played a large role in financing railroads and other companies. He worked with Andrew Carnegie to form U.S. Steel in 1901. At the time, it was the most valuable company in the world.

John D. Rockefeller (1839–1937) built a refinery to turn raw oil into usable fuel. He went on to create the largest oil company in the country.

Theodore Roosevelt (1858–1919) was the 26th U.S. president. He was sometimes called the "trust buster" because of his efforts to break up large companies that controlled an industry.

Franklin D. Roosevelt (1882–1945) was the 32nd president of the United States. He served for 12 years, longer than any other president. He is best known for the New Deal, a series of government programs designed to ease the harsh effects of the Great Depression.

Ronald Reagan

Ronald Reagan (1911–2004) was the 40th U.S. president. He fought for lower taxes and for the government to have a smaller role in the economy. He wanted the free market to be as free as possible, to increase profits and create jobs.

Bill Gates (1955–) had a childhood interest in programming computers. With his friend Paul Allen, he created a program for one of the first personal computers and then founded Microsoft. The company's software is now used on computers around the globe, and Gates is one of the world's richest people.

Bill Gates

Steve Jobs (1955–2011) created one of the first personal computers with his partner, Steve Wozniak. As head of Apple Inc., Jobs sold products with a simple, sleek design that were unlike anything his competitors offered.

TIMELINE

1733
Great Britain enacts a duty on molasses in the American colonies.

1765
The Stamp Act requires Americans to pay a tax on most paper goods they use.

1776
The American colonies declare their independence from Great Britain; Adam Smith publishes *The Wealth of Nations*.

1837
A recession limits the amount of money available for banks to loan.

1848
Gold is discovered in California, drawing investors and entrepreneurs west.

1873
A recession starts that lasts several years and leads to violence during railroad strikes.

1890
Congress passes the Sherman Anti-Trust Act.

1933
President Franklin D. Roosevelt begins a series of government programs called the New Deal.

1939
Germany invades Poland, starting World War II.

1970s
Rising oil prices fuel inflation; the first personal computers appear.

1789

Alexander Hamilton becomes the first secretary of the treasury.

1790

Samuel Slater and Moses Brown open the first textile mill in the United States.

1793

A group of investors form what later becomes the New York Stock Exchange.

1893

A depression begins, leading to high unemployment for several years.

1902

President Theodore Roosevelt begins the era of "trust busting."

1929

The stock market crashes, beginning the Great Depression.

1980

Ronald Reagan is elected president.

Late 1990s

Many Internet companies go out of business.

2007

A drastic fall in the value of homes leads to another recession.

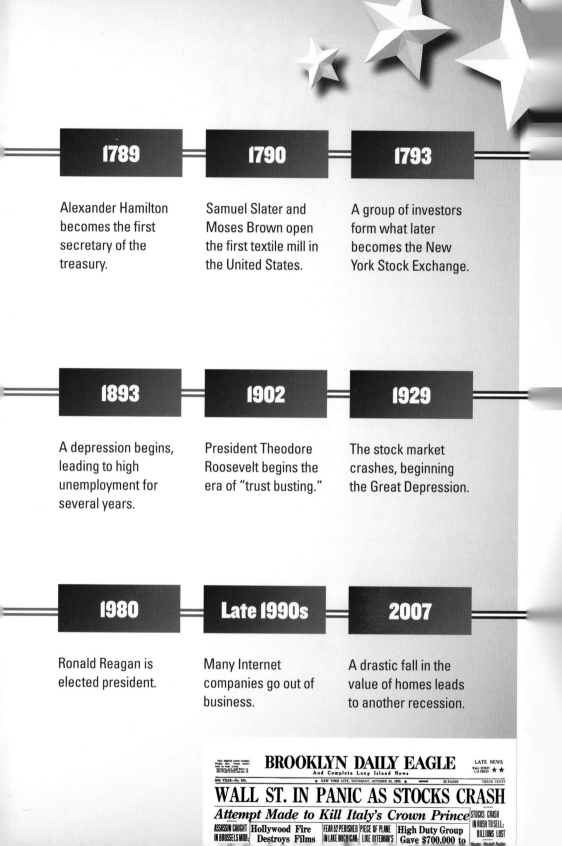

LIVING HISTORY

Primary sources provide firsthand evidence about a topic. Witnesses to a historical event create primary sources. They include autobiographies, newspaper reports of the time, oral histories, photographs, and memoirs. A secondary source analyzes primary sources, and is one step or more removed from the event. Secondary sources include textbooks, encyclopedias, and commentaries. To view the following primary and secondary sources, go to www.factsfornow.scholastic.com. Enter the keywords **American Capitalism** and look for the Living History logo Σ¡.

Σ¡ **Edison's Patent Application** Thomas Edison invented several devices that changed American life forever, including the motion picture camera and the lightbulb.

Σ¡ **"Only a Workingman's Child"** Many popular songs of the late 1800s dealt with the poor economy and the struggles of workers. Ned Straight's "Only a Workingman's Child" tells the story of a young girl who works to help her family.

Σ¡ **Steve Jobs's Stanford Speech** Steve Jobs was an inventor who helped create and popularize the personal computer. In 2005, he gave a speech to the new graduates of Stanford University.

Σ¡ *The Wealth of Nations* Economist Adam Smith's *An Inquiry into the Nature and Causes of the Wealth of Nations* was a major influence on the U.S. economy in the years following the Revolutionary War.

RESOURCES

Books

Espejo, Roman, ed. *Consumerism*. Detroit: Greenhaven Press, 2010.

Furgang, Kathy. *How the Stock Market Works*. New York: Rosen Publishing, 2011.

The Great Depression. Chicago: World Book, 2011.

Simons, Rae. *All About Money: The History, Culture, and Meaning of Modern Finance*. Broomall, PA: Mason Crest, 2011.

Visit this Scholastic Web site for more information on American Capitalism:
www.factsfornow.scholastic.com
Enter the keywords **American Capitalism**

GLOSSARY

commercial (kuh-MUR-shuhl) having to do with buying and selling things

consumers (kuhn-SOO-murz) people who buy and use products and services

debt (DET) money or something else that someone owes

dividends (DIV-uh-dendz) shares of the money earned by an investment or a business

domestic (duh-MES-tik) within your own country

economy (i-KAHN-uh-mee) the system of buying, selling, making things, and managing money in a place

entrepreneurs (ahn-truh-pruh-NURZ) people who start businesses and find new ways to make money

exports (EK-sports) products sent to another country to be sold there

imported (im-PORT-id) brought in from a foreign country

inflation (in-FLAY-shuhn) a general increase in prices, causing money to be worth less

interest (IN-trest) a fee charged by moneylenders; a sum paid by a bank or other company for holding and using a consumer's money

monopolies (muh-NAHP-uh-leez) the complete possession or control of the supply of a product or service

mortgages (MOHR-gi-jiz) loan agreements to buy property; the property goes to the lender if the loan is not repaid

speculations (spek-yuh-LAY-shuhnz) investments in things that are risky, such as businesses or stocks

textiles (TEK-stylz) fabrics or cloths that have been woven or knitted

Page numbers in *italics* indicate illustrations.

ABOUT THE AUTHOR

Michael Burgan is the author of more than 250 books for children and young adults, both fiction and nonfiction. His works include several books on U.S. economic history. A graduate of the University of Connecticut, Burgan is also a produced playwright. He lives in Santa Fe, New Mexico.